Joh. Seb.
BACH

MAGNIFICAT
BWV 243
Edited by
Karl Straube

Vocal Score
Klavierauszug

SERENISSIMA MUSIC, INC.

CONTENTS

ORCHESTRA

2 Flutes, 2 Oboes, Bassoon
3 Trumpets, Timpani
Basso Continuo (Organ, Harpsichord)
Violin I, Violin II, Violoncello, Double Bass

Premeire: Christmas Day, 1723
Leipzig, Thomaskirche
Soli, Chorus and Orchestra, conducted by the composer
Duration: ca. 33 minutes

Complete orchestral parts compatible with this vocal score are available

MAGNIFICAT
BWV 243
1. Magnificat Anima Mea

Johann Sebastian Bach
Piano reduction by Karl Straube

Tromp. dazu
Fl.u.Ob.
Fl.u.Str.
Ob.
mf
Holzbl.
Tr I.
Vl.
Ob.
f mp
Vl.u.Br. unisono (ohne Bässe!)
Tromp.
pocof cresc.
B
Vl.
Ob.
Tromp.
ff
Fl.
Ob. u. Vl. dazu
Tromp.
senza ritenuto

Soprano I
Ma - - - - gni - fi - cat, ma - gni - fi - cat, ma - gni - fi - cat,
Soprano II
Ma - - - - gni - fi - cat, ma - gni - fi - cat, ma - gni - fi - cat,
Alto
Ma - - - - - - - gni - fi - cat, ma - gni - fi - cat,
Tenor
Ma - - - - - - - gni - fi - cat, ma - gni - fi - cat,
Bass
Ma - gni - fi - cat, ma - gni - fi - cat,
Fl.
Ob.
Org.
poco f
Vcl. u. K. B.
Tromp.
C
marc.
ma - - - gni - fi - cat, ma - - gni - fi - cat a - ni - ma
espr.
ma - - - - gni - fi - cat, a - - - ni - ma me - a,
ma - - gni - fi - cat, ma - gni - fi - cat, ma - gni - - fi - cat, ma -
ma - - gni - fi - cat, ma - gni - fi - cat, ma - gni - - fi - cat, ma -
ma - gni - fi - cat, ma - - - - - - - - - -
Org.
Tromp. I
Vl.
Fl.
Ob.
poco f
Br.
Vcl. u. K. B

39
leggiero
me - a, a - - - - - - - - - - - - - ni-ma me - a, a - - ni-ma
ma - - gni - fi - cat, ma - - gni - fi - cat a - ni-ma, a - - - - ni-ma
gni - fi-cat, ma - - - - gni - fi-cat, ma - - - - gni - fi-cat a - - ni-ma
gni - fi-cat, ma - - - - gni - fi-cat, ma - - - - gni - fi-cat a - - ni-ma
f
gni-fi-cat a - - ni-ma me - a, a - - ni-ma me - a, a - - ni-ma
39
mf
Tromp I.
marcato
f
42
cresc.
me - a, a - - - ni-ma me - a Do - - - - - - - - - - - - - mi -
me - a, a - - - - ni-ma me - a, a - - - - ni-ma me - a Do - - mi - -
me - a, a - - - ni-ma me - a, a - - - - ni-ma me - a Do - - mi - -
me - a, ma - gni - fi - cat a - - - ni - ma me - a Do - - - - mi -
me - a, a - - - ni-ma me - a, a - - - ni - ma me - a Do - mi -
42
(tr)

45
num, ma - gni - fi-cat, ma - gni - fi-cat,
num, ma - gni - fi-cat, ma - gni - fi-cat,
num, ma - gni - fi-cat, ma - gni - fi-cat, ma - gni - fi-cat,
num, ma - gni - fi-cat, ma - gni - fi-cat, ma - gni - fi-cat,
num, ma - gni - fi-cat, ma - gni - fi-cat,
45
Org.
Fl.
Tromp.
Str.
Vcl. u. K. B.
49 D
ma - gni - fi-cat, ma - gni - fi-cat, ma -
leggiero
ma - gni - fi-cat, ma - gni - fi-cat,
ma - gni - fi-cat,
marc.
49 D
Org.
Fl.
Ob.
Vl. u. Br.
Vcl. u. K. B

53
gni - fi - cat, ma - gni - fi - cat, ma - gni - fi - cat, ma -
ma - gni - fi - cat, ma - gni - fi - cat, ma - gni - fi - cat, ma -
legg.
marc.
ma - gni - fi - cat, ma -
marc.
ma - gni - fi - cat,
ma -
57
gni - fi - cat, ma - gni - fi - cat, ma - gni - fi - cat, ma - gni - fi -
gni - fi - cat, ma - gni - fi - cat, ma - gni - fi - cat, ma - gni - fi - cat, ma - gni - fi -
gni - fi - cat, ma - gni - fi - cat, ma - gni - fi - cat, ma - gni - fi -
ma - gni - fi - cat, ma - gni - fi - cat, ma - gni - fi -
gni - fi - cat, ma - gni - fi - cat, ma - gni - fi -
cresc.
marc.
Tromp.
Fl.u.Ob.
Vl.u.Br.
Tromp.

61
E
ff
mf
cat, ma - gni - fi - cat,
cat, ma - gni - fi - cat,
f
cat, ma - - - gni - fi - cat, ma - gni - fi - cat, ma -
cat, ma - - - gni - fi - cat, ma - - - gni - fi - cat, ma -
f marc.
cat, ma - gni - fi - cat, ma - - - gni - fi - cat, ma -
Ob.
Fl.
mp
65
ma - - - gni - fi - cat, ma - gni - fi - cat, ma - gni - fi - cat, ma -
legg.
ma - - - gni - fi - cat, ma - gni - fi - cat, ma - - gni - fi - cat a - ni - ma
gni - fi - cat, ma - gni - fi - cat a - - - ni - ma me - a,
gni - fi - cat, ma - gni - fi - cat, ma - gni - fi - cat, ma -
ff marc.
gni - fi - cat, ma - gni - fi - cat, ma - - - - - - -
Str.
poco f
Tromp.
Fl. I u. Ob. I
Fl. II u. Ob. II

69
gni - - fi-cat, ma - - - gni - fi-cat, ma - - - - gni - fi-cat a - - ni-ma
legg.
me - a, a - - - - - - - - - - - ni-ma me - a, a - - ni-ma
ma - - - gni - fi - cat, ma - - - gni-fi-cat a-ni-ma, a - - - ni-ma
gni - - fi-cat, ma - - - gni - fi-cat, ma - - - - gni - fi-cat a - ni-ma
f
gni-fi-cat a - - ni-ma me-a, a - - ni-ma me-a, a - - ni-ma
69
Fl.u.Vl.
Tromp.I
Tromp.
poco a poco cresc.
72
cresc.
me-a, ma-gni - fi - cat a - - - ni - ma me-a Do - - - mi-
cresc.
me-a, a - - ni-ma me-a Do - - - - - - - - - mi-
cresc.
me-a, a - - - ni-ma me-a, a - - - ni-ma me-a Do - - mi -
cresc.
me-a, a - - ni-ma me-a, a - - - ni-ma me-a Do - - - - mi-
cresc.
me-a, a - - ni-ma me-a, a-ni-ma me - - - a Do-mi-
senza rit.
72

F
fff
num.
Ob.
ff
mf
Fl. u. Str.
Tromp. dazu
Holzbl.
Vl.
Tr. I.
Ob.
f
mp
Vl. u. Br. unisone (ohne Bässe!)
Tromp.
poco f
cresc.
Vl.
Ob.
Tromp.
ff
Fl.
Ob. u. Vl. dazu
Tromp.
fff
attacca
Nº 2

2. Et Exultavit

Et ex - ul - ta - vit spi - ri - tus

senza ripieni *)

me - us,

*) In den Einzelgesängen ist das Orchester in: Tutti und: senza ripieni, d. h. ungefähr in: großes Orchester und: kleine (Kammer-) Besetzung geteilt; die letztere gibt die eigentliche Begleitung.

A
p
et ex - ul - ta - vit spi - ri - tus me - us, et ex - ul -
senza ripieni
poco a
ta - vit spi - ri - tus me - us, et ex - ul - ta - - -
poco cresc.
f
- - - - - - - - - - vit spi - ri - tus me -
poco f
us in De - - - - - o sa - lu - ta - - - -
p

40
p
cresc.
-ri, sa - lu - ta - - - - - - - - - - - - - -
Vl.I
mp
mp
45
poco ritenuto
f
espr.
- - - - - - - ri me - o, in De - o sa - lu - ta - - ri me -
mf
51 B a tempo
o.
Tutti
p
poco a poco
cresc.
57
mp
p
Et ex - ul - ta - vit spi - ri - tus me - us in
senza ripieni
f
p

63
un poco rit.
f espressivo
De - - - o sa - lu - ta - - - - ri, sa - lu - ta - - - - - -
Vl. I
69
C
a tempo
p
im Ausdruck steigern
- ri me - - o, in De - - - o, sa - lu - ta - ri,
poco a poco cresc. - - - -
75
f
p
espr.
poco rit. -
in De - o sa - - lu - ta - - ri me - - o, in De - o sa - lu - ta -
poco f
80
D
a tempo
ri me - - o.
Tutti
86
rallentando - -
più f
ff
attacca No 3

3. Quia Respexit

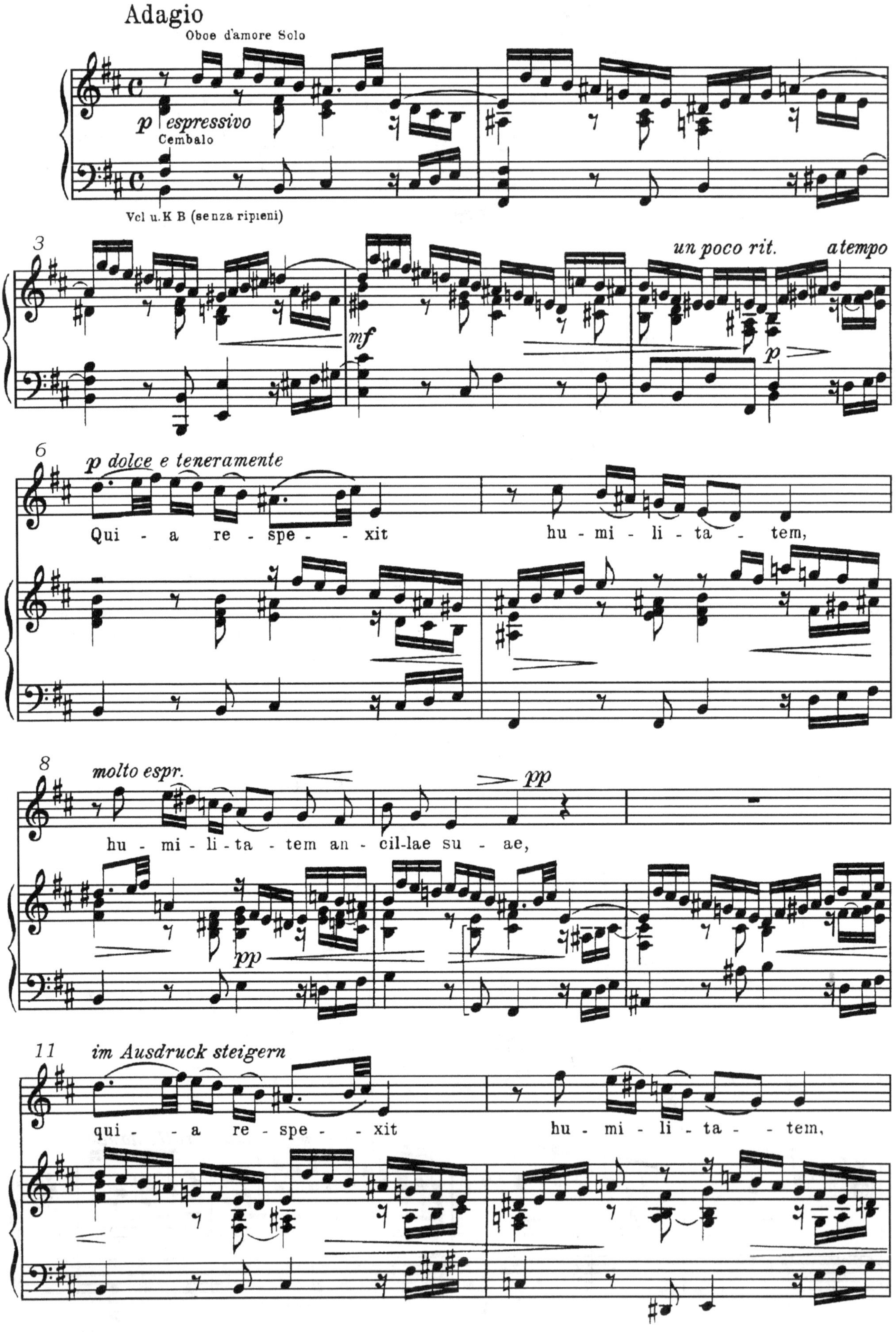

A Più Adagio
tr pp
rall.
hu-mi-li-ta - tem an - cil-lae su - ae:
p
Poco più Andante.
rit.
ec-ce, ec - ce,
mf
ec - ce, ec - ce,
mp
f
ec-ce e-nim ex hoc be -
a - tam, ec-ce e - nim ex hoc be - a - tam, be - a - - - - -
- tam me di - cent, be-a - - - - tam, be - a - - - - - - - tam me di -
ritardando
espr.

4. Omnes Generationes

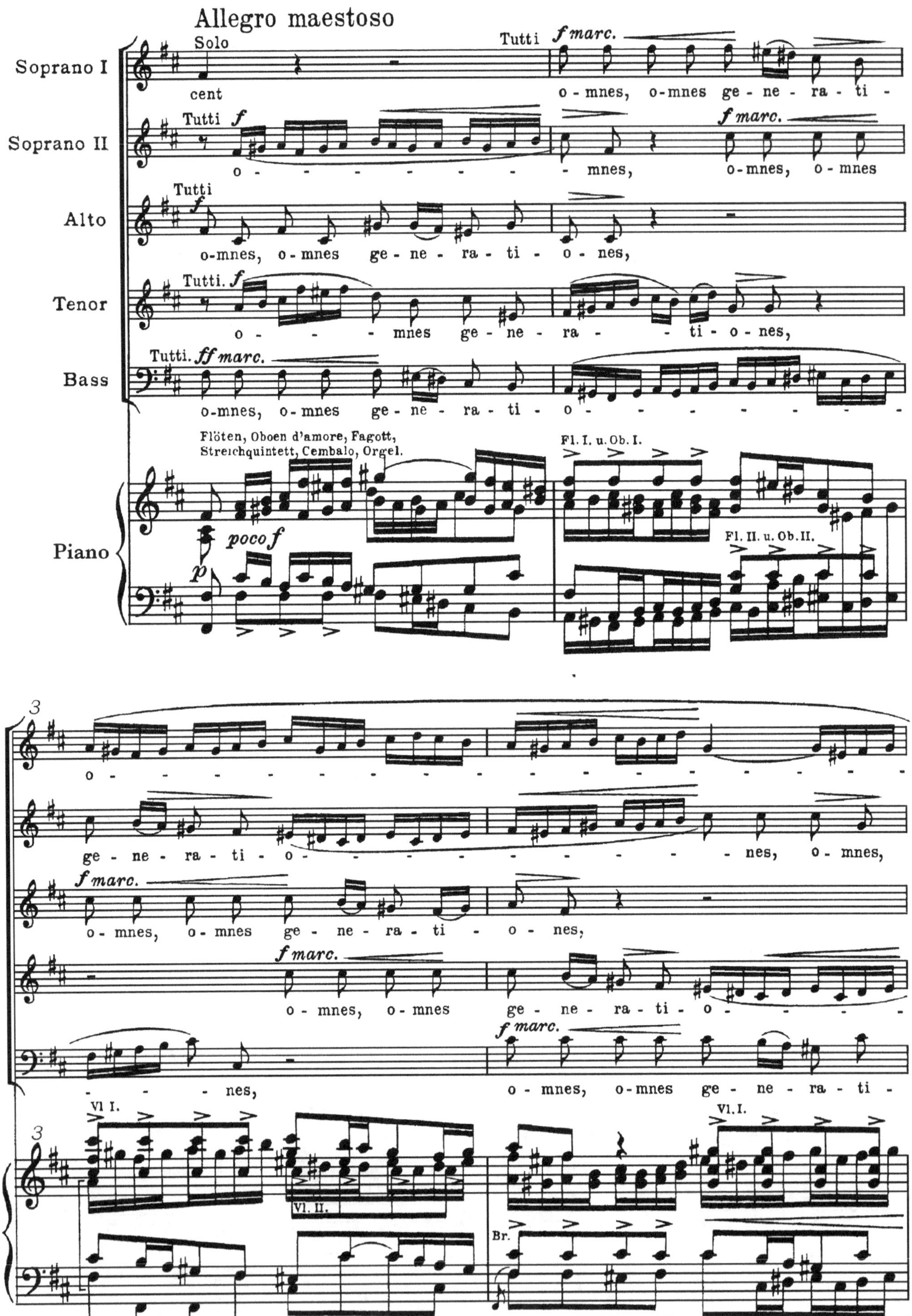

5
f marc.
nes, o-mnes, o-mnes ge-ne-ra-ti-
marc.
o- mnes, o-mnes ge-ne-ra-ti-o-
f marc.
o-mnes, o-mnes ge-ne-ra-ti-o-
nes,
cresc.
ff marc.
o-nes, o- mnes, o-mnes
5
Fl. I. u. Ob. I.
Br.
Fl. II. u. Ob. II.
f
poco a poco cresc.
7
cresc.
ff marc.
o- nes, o- mnes, o-mnes
ff marc.
nes, o-mnes ge-ne-ra-ti-
ff marc.
nes, o-mnes ge-ne-ra-ti-o-
ff
marc.
o- mnes, o-mnes ge-ne-ra-ti-o-
ge-ne-ra-ti-o-
7
Vl. I.
Vl. II.
Fl. II. u. Ob. II.
Fl. I. u. Ob. I.

A
ff
f marc.
ge - ne - ra - ti - o - - - nes, o - mnes, o - mnes
o - - - - - - - - - - - nes,
nes,
nes,
ff marc.
nes, o-mnes, o - mnes ge - ne - ra - ti -
Vl. I
Fl. I. u. Ob. I.
mf
legg.
ge - ne - ra - ti - o - - - - - - - - nes,
f marc.
o - mnes, o - mnes ge - ne - ra - ti - o - - - - -
o - mnes, o - mnes
o - mnes, o - mnes ge - ne - ra - ti - o - - - - -
o - - - - - - nes,
o - mnes, o - mnes ge - ne - ra - ti -
Vl. II.
Fl. II. u. Ob. II.
Br
Vl. I.

13
f marc.
legg.
o - mnes, o - mnes ge - ne - ra - ti - o - - - - - - - -
f marc.
- - - - - - - nes, o - mnes, o - mnes ge - ne - ra - ti -
ge - ne - ra - ti - o - - - - - - - - - - - - - - nes,
f marc.
- - nes, o - mnes, o - mnes ge - ne - ra - ti - o - - - - -
f marc.
o - - - - - - - - - - - nes, o - mnes, o - mnes
13
Fl. I. u. Ob. I.
Vl. II.
Fl. II. u. Ob. II.
f Br.
15
f
ff marc.
- - nes, o - mnes ge - ne - ra - ti - o - nes, o - mnes, o - mnes
ff marc.
o - - - - - - - - - - - - nes, o - mnes ge - ne - ra - ti -
ff marc.
o - mnes, o - mnes ge - ne - ra - ti - o - - - - -
- - - - - - - - - - - - - nes,
ge - ne - ra - ti - o - - - - - - - - - - - - - - -
15
Fl. I. u. Ob. I.
Vl. I.
poco a poco cresc. -
Fl. II. u. Ob. II.
Fl. I. u. Ob. I.

ff marc.
ge - ne - ra - ti - o - - - - - - nes, o - - - mnes, o - mnes
ff marc.
o - - - nes, o - mnes, o - mnes ge - ne - ra - ti -
- - - - - - - - - - - - - - - - nes,
ff marc.
o - mnes, o - mnes ge - ne - ra - ti - o - - - - - - - - - -
ff marc.
- nes, o - mnes, o - mnes ge - ne - ra - ti - o - - - -
Vl. II.
Br.
Fl. II. u. Ob. II.
Fl. I. u. Ob. I.
ff
ge - ne - ra - ti - o - - - - - - - nes, ge - ne - ra - ti - o -
ff
o - - - - - - - - - - - nes, ge - ne - ra - ti - o -
ff marc.
f
o - mnes, o - mnes ge - ne - ra - ti - o - - - - - - - -
fff marc.
- nes, o - mnes ge - ne - ra - ti - o -
cresc.
fff marc.
- - - - - nes, o - mnes ge - ne - ra - ti - o - - - -
Vl. I.
Br.
Vl. II.

attacca № 5.

5. Quia Fecit Mihi Magna

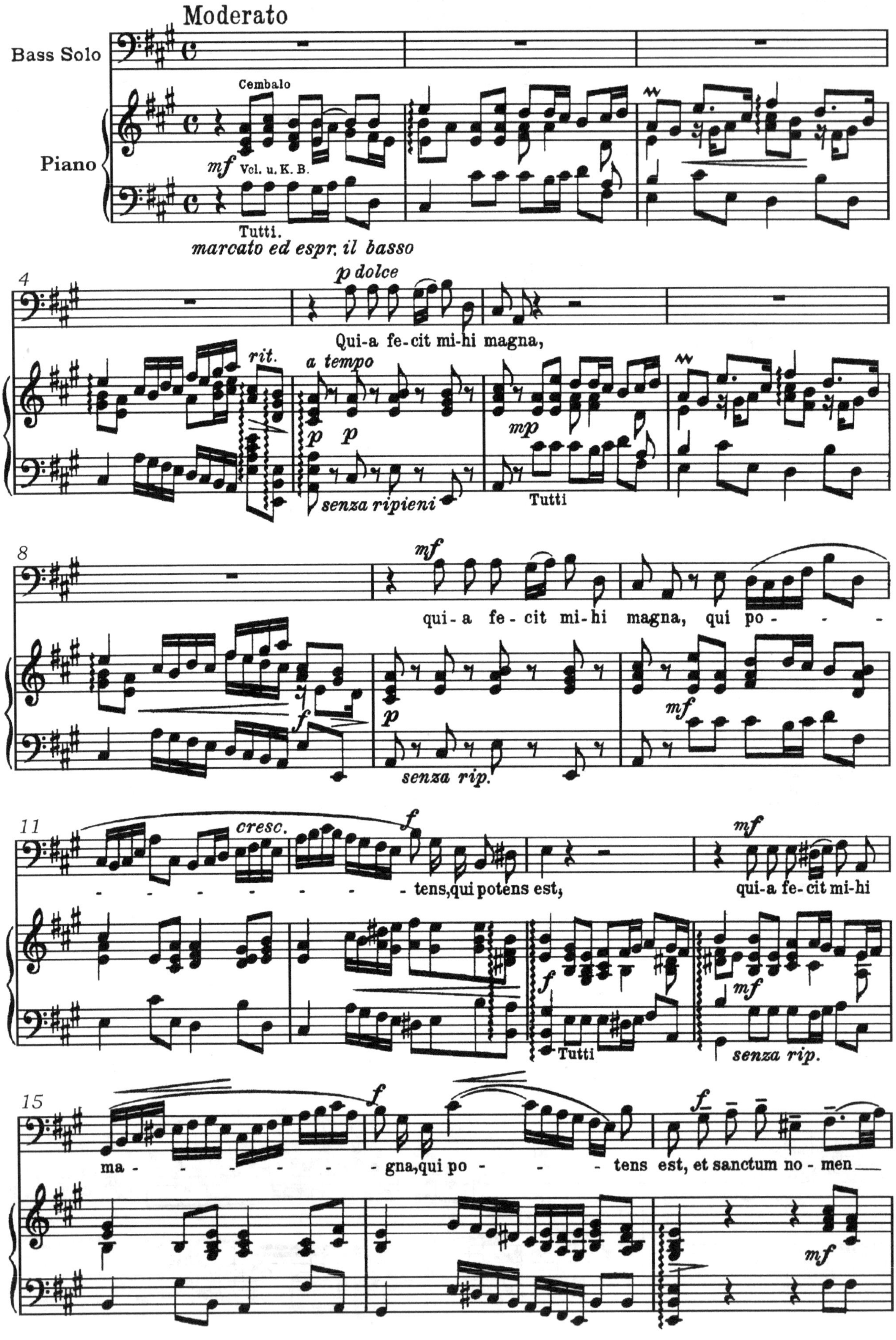

e - jus, et san - - - - - ctum no-men, et sanctum no-men e - jus, san - -

- - ctum nomen e-jus, sanctum no - men __ e - jus, et san - - - ctum no - men e - -

jus; qui - a fe - cit mi - hi ma - - gna, qui po - - tens

est, et san - - - - - ctum no-men. san - ctum no-men e - jus.

attacca № 6

6. Et Misericordia

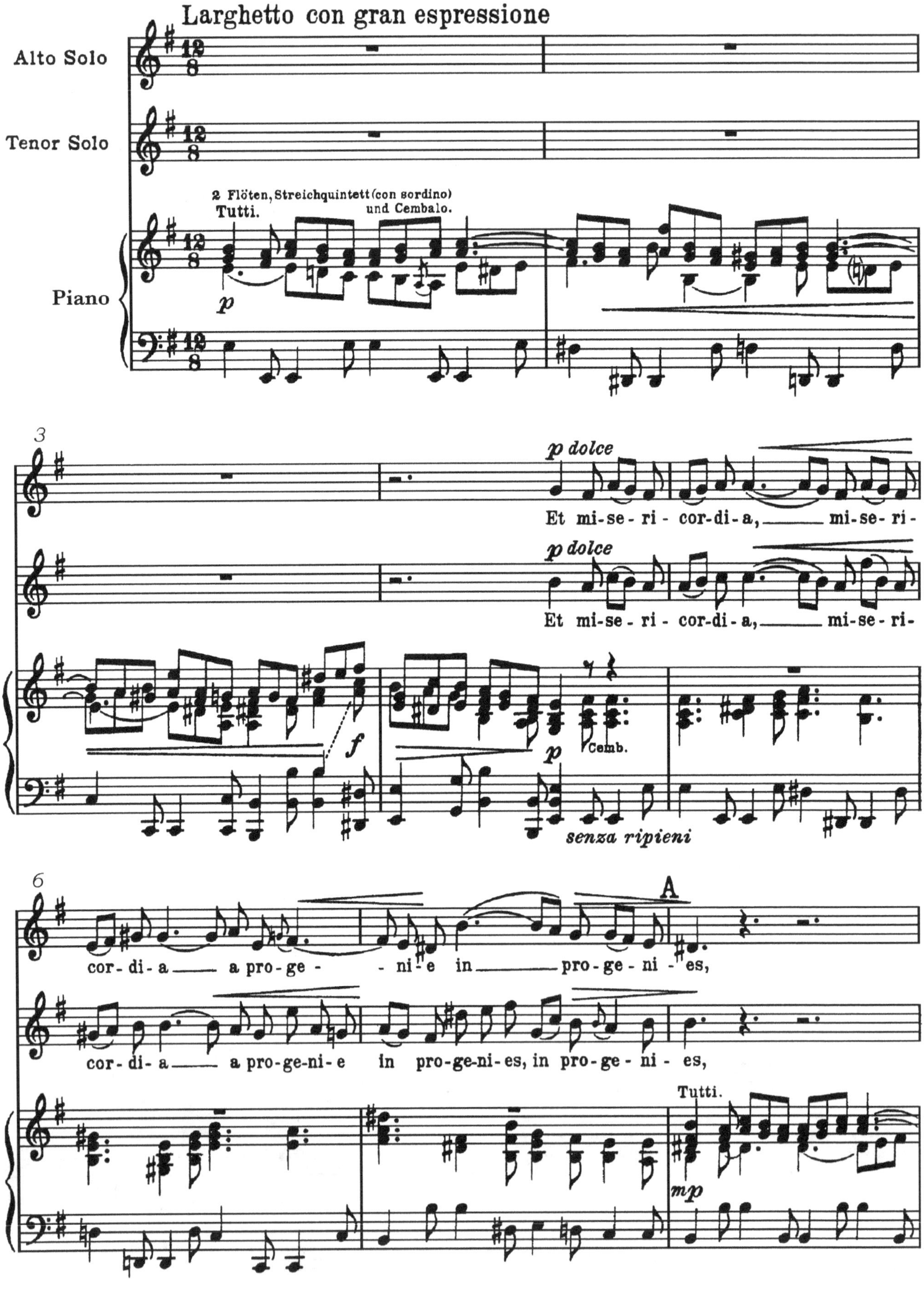

9
mf
et mi-se-ri-
mf
et mi-se-ri-
f
mp
12
cor-di-a, mi-se-ri - cor- di- a a pro-ge-ni-e in pro-ge-ni-es, in pro-ge- ni-
cor- di-a, mi-se- ri - cor- di- a a pro-ge - - ni- e in pro-ge- ni-
senza ripieni
espr.
mf
mf
15 B
p
es ti-men - ti-bus e-um, ti- men - - ti-bus
p
es ti-men - - ti-bus e - um, ti-men - ti-bus
mf
mf
p
mp

18
e - um,
et mi-se-ri-
e - um,
et mi-se-ri-
Tutti.
mf
f
21
cor-di-a, mi-se-ri - cor - di-a a pro ge-ni-e in pro-ge-ni-es, in pro-ge - ni-
cor-di-a, mi-se-ri - cor - di-a a pro-ge - - ni-e in pro-ge - ni-
senza ripieni
espr.
mf
mf
24
C
p
es ti-men - ti-bus e - um, ti-men - - ti-bus
p
es ti-men - - ti-bus e - um, ti-men - - ti-bus
f
f
p
mf
f

e - um, ti - men - - ti - bus, ti - men - - - - ti - bus, ti-

e - um, ti - men - - ti - bus, ti - men - - - - ti - bus, ti-

men-ti-bus e - um, ti - men - - - ti-bus e - um.

men-ti-bus e - um, ti - men - - ti-bus e - um.

attacca Nº 7.

7. Fecit Potentiam

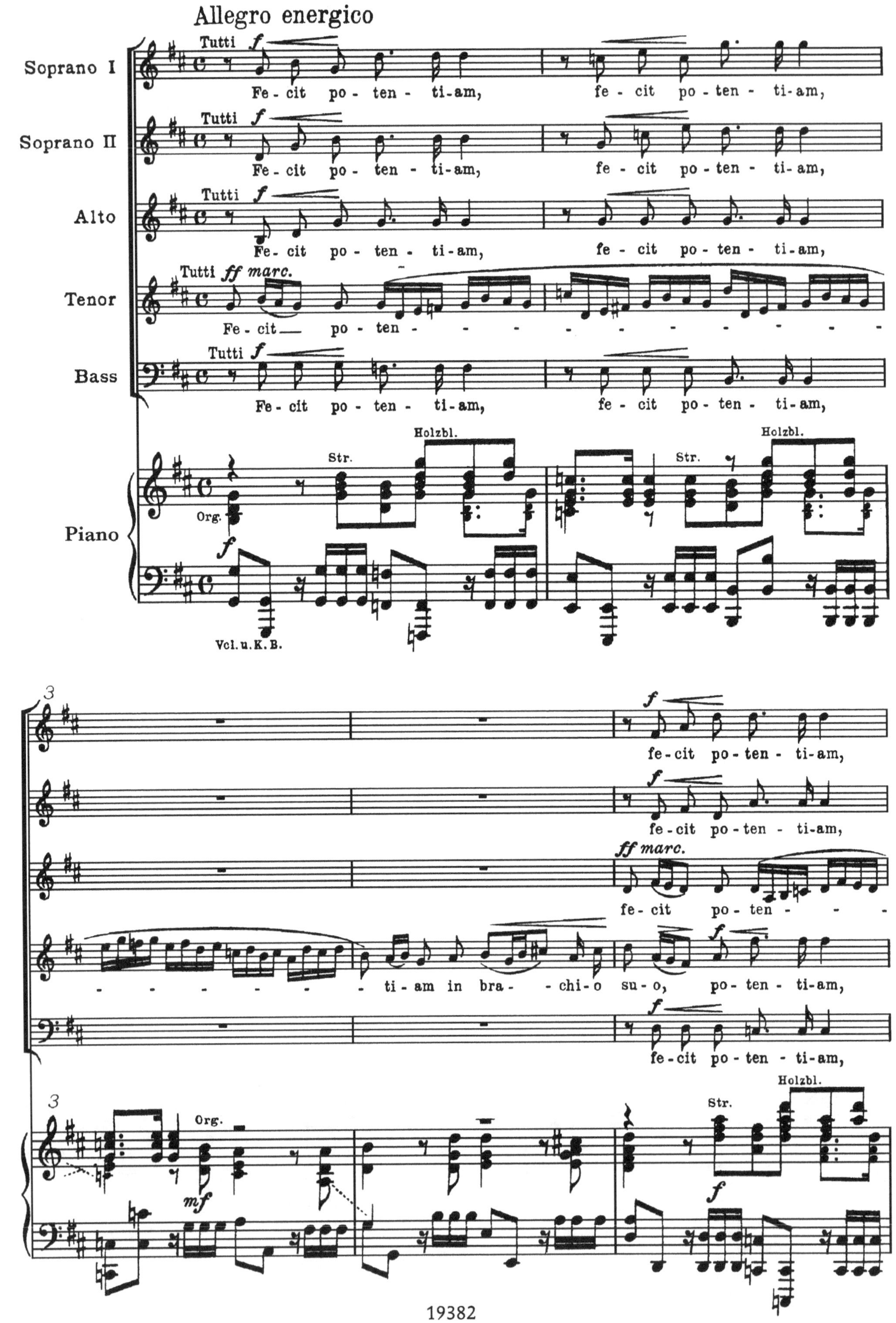

6
fe-cit po-ten-ti-am,
fe-cit po-ten-ti-am,
ti-am, in bra - chi-o
fe-cit po-ten-ti-am, in bra - chi-o su - o, di-sper
fe-cit po-ten-ti-am,
6
Holzbl.
Str
Org.
mf
9
f
fe-cit po-ten-ti-am, fe-cit po-ten-ti-am,
ff marc.
fe-cit po-ten
su-o, po-ten-ti-am, fe-cit po-ten-ti-am, in bra - chi-o su
marc.
sit, fe-cit po-ten-ti-am, fe-cit po-ten-ti-am, di-sper - sit, disper-sit,
fe-cit po-ten-ti-am, fe-cit po-ten-ti-am,
9
Holzbl.
Str.
Holzbl.
Str.
Org.
mf

12
A
f
fe - cit po - ten - ti - am, fe - cit po - ten - ti - am,
- ti - am in bra - chi - o su - o, po - ten - ti - am, fe - cit po - ten - ti - am,
o, di - sper - - sit, fe - cit po - ten - ti - am, fe - cit po - ten - ti - am, di -
marc.
di - sper - - sit, fe - cit po - ten - ti - am, fe - cit po - ten - ti - am, di -
ff marc.
fe - cit po - ten - - - - -
Str.
Holzbl.
12
A
Tromp.
ff
15
ff marc.
fe - cit po - ten - -
in bra - chi - o su - o, di - sper - - sit, fe - cit po - ten - ti - am,
marc.
sper - - sit, disper - sit, di - sper - - sit, fe - cit po - ten - ti - am,
marc.
sper - sit, di - sper - sit, di - spersit, di - sper - - sit, fe - cit po - ten - ti - am,
- - - - - - - ti - am in bra - chi - o su - o, fe - cit po - ten - ti - am,
Str
15
Org.
f
Tromp.
ff
Holzbl.

18
- - - - - - - - - - - - - - - ti-am in bra- -chi-o
marc.
fe-cit po-ten-ti-am, di-sper- - -sit, di-sper-sit, di-sper- - - - -
marc. sempre
fe-cit po-ten-ti-am, di-sper-sit, di-sper-sit, di-sper-sit, di-sper- - -
marc. sempre
fe-cit po-ten-ti-am, di-sper-sit, di-sper-sit, di-sper-sit, di-sper-sit,
fe-cit po-ten-ti-am, in bra- -chi-o su- -o, di-sper- - - - -
18
Org.
f
21 B
su-o, po-ten-ti-am, fe-cit po-ten-ti-am,
-sit, fe-cit po-ten-ti-am, fe-cit po-ten-ti-am, di-
-sit, fe-cit po-ten-ti-am, fe-cit po-ten-ti-am, di-
sempre
fe-cit po-ten-ti-am, fe-cit po-ten-ti-am, di-
-sit, fe-cit po-ten-ti-am, fe-cit po-ten-ti-am,
Tromp. II.
Tromp. III.
21 B
Tromp. I. u. Fl.
ff
Str. u. Ob.

*) In der Bachausgabe steht cis, sämtliche Parallelstellen fordern c.

27
Adagio.
cresc.
fff
di-sper-sit su-per-bos men - te cor - dis
spersit, di - sper - sit su-per-bos men - te cor - dis
sper-sit, di-sper-sit su-per-bos men - te cor - dis
di-sper-sit, su-per-bos men - te cor - dis
Tromp.
Fl.
Str.
l.H.
Holzbl. dazu
ff
Tutti ohne Tromp. u. Pauk.
31
pp
cresc.
ritenuto
su - - - - - i, men - te cor - dis su - - - - - - i.
Tromp.
mp cresc. molto
Tromp. I.
tr
l.H.
Pk.

attacca No 8

8. Deposuit

Appassionato, ma non troppo allegro

24
cresc.
ff
vit hu mi
Tutti
crescendo
ff
28
les,
f
32
B
f
de - po -
(tr)
mf senza ripieni
36
su - it, de - po - su - it po - ten -
marc.
poco f
marc.
40
tes de se - de, et ex - al - ta -
mf
f
mf crescendo

Un pochettino più tranquillo
vit et ex-al - ta - vit hu - mi -
les, et ex-al-ta-
vit hu - mi - les.
Tempo I
a tempo
Tutti.
un poco rit.
più f
crescendo
senza rit.
attacca No 9.

9. Esurientes

Amabile e con tenerezza

2 Flöten, Violoncelli, K.B. (senza ripieni) und Cembalo.

p dolce e grazioso

(pizz.)
una corda

E - su - ri - en - tes im - ple - - vit bo - nis,

e - su - ri - en - tes im - ple - - vit bo - nis, et di - vi - tes di - mi - sit, et

19382

13

poco f *p*

di - vi - tes di - mi - sit, di - mi - sit in - a - nes, et di - vi - tes di - mi - sit in-

16

tr **B**

a - - nes, di - mi - sit in - a - nes;

p dolce e grazioso

19

p

e - su - ri - en - tes im-

22

tr *mp* *mf* *p*

ple - - vit bo - nis, e - su - ri - en - tes im - ple - vit bo - -

25

p **C**

- nis, im - ple - - - - -

28
- - - - - - - - - - - - - - - - - - - vit
2 Fl. unisono
31
bo-nis, et di-vi-tes di - mi - sit, et di - vi-tes di - mi-sit, di-mi - - sit
espr.
34
D
un poco rall.
in - a - nes, di-mi-sit in - a - nes, di-mi-sit in-a - - nes.
un poco rallentando
Tempo I.
p dolce e grazioso
37
40
ritenuto

10. Suscepit Israel

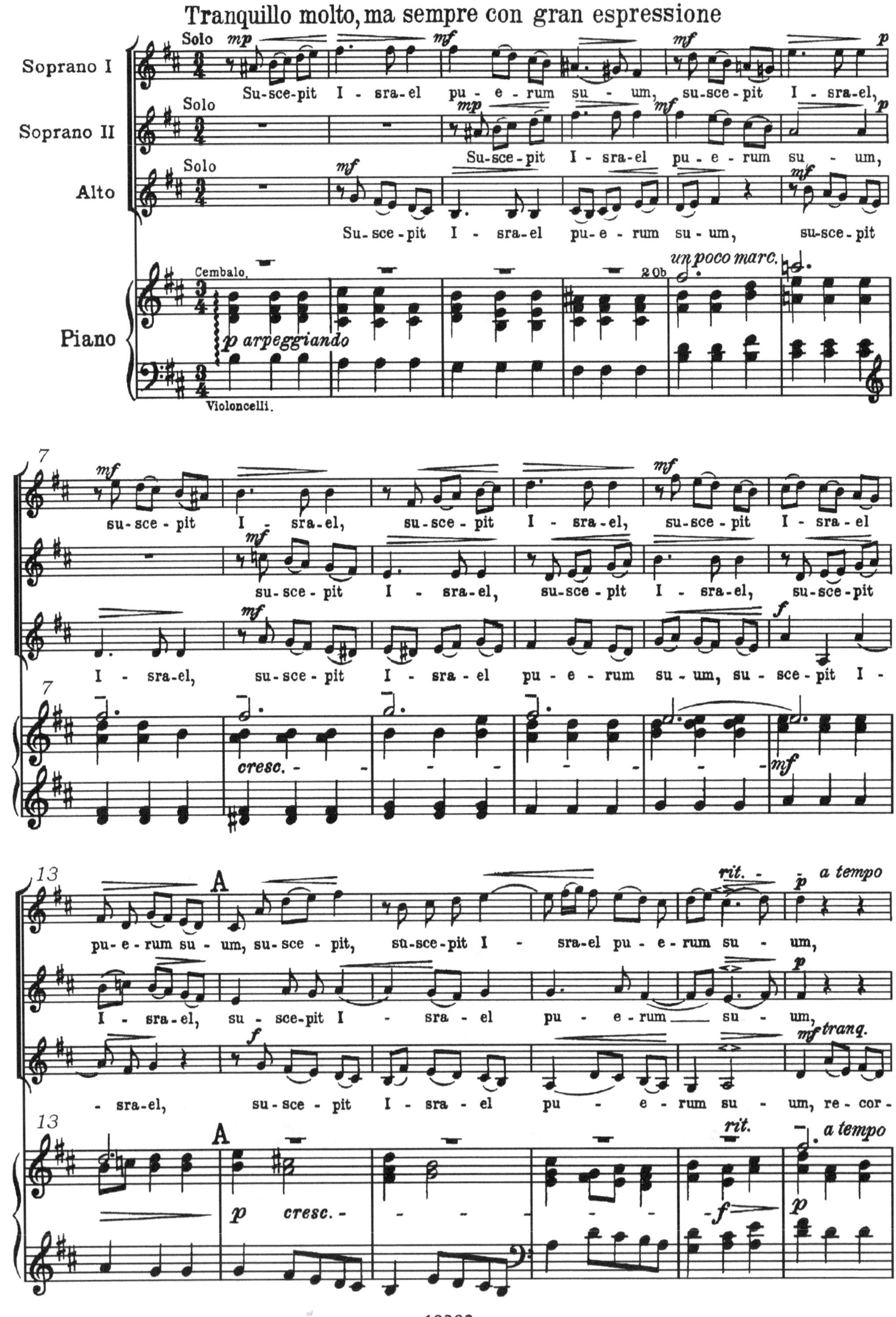

19
mf tranq.
espr. molto
re - cor - da - tus mi - se - ri - cor - - - - - - - - - - - - - -
mf tranq.
re - cor - da - tus mi - se - ri - cor - - - - - - - - - di -
p
espr
da - tus mi - se - ri - cor - - - - - - - - - - - - - - -
19
pp poco a poco cresc.
25
f
p
f espr.
B
- di - ae su - ae, re - cor - da - tus mi - - se - ri - cor - -
f espr.
espr.
p
ae, re - cor - da - tus mi - se - ri - cor - di - ae, mi - se - ri -
f
f espr.
p
espr.
- - di - ae, re - cor - da - tus mi - se - ri - cor - - - - - - di -
25
B
f
31
f espr.
rit.
pp
- di - ae su - ae, mi - se - ri - cor - - - - - - di - ae su - ae.
f espr.
pp
cor - - - - - - - - - - di - ae su - - - - ae.
p f
espr.
p
ae, mi - se - ri - cor - - - di - ae, mi - se - ri - cor - di - ae su - ae.
31
p
f
dim. e rit.
ppp

11. Sicut Locutus

14
cu - - tus est ad pa-tres no - - stros, A-bra-ham et se-mi-ni e - jus in
ham et se-mi-ni e - jus in se - cu - la, in se - cu - - la, in se - -
cu - tus est in se - cu - la, si - cut lo - cu - tus est ad pa-tres
cut lo - cu - tus est ad pa-tres no - - stros, si-cut lo - cu - tus est in
mf
f marc.
cresc.
marc.
20
A
Tutti.
Si - cut lo - cu - - tus est ad pa-tres no - - stros, A-bra-ham et se-mi-ni
se - cu - la, A-bra-ham et se-mi-ni e - jus in se - cu - la, si-cut lo - cu - - tus
- - cu - la, si - cut lo - cu - - tus
no - stros, si-cut lo - cu - tus est in se - cu - la,
se - cu - la,
p
f
mp

27
e - jus in se - cu - la, si-cut lo - cu - tus est in se - cu - la,
est ad pa-tres no-stros in se - cu - la, ad pa-tres no - stros, si-
est ad pa-tres no - - stros, A-bra-ham et se-mi-ni e - jus in se - cu - la, si-cut lo-
si - cut lo - cu - - tus est ad pa-tres no - stros, A-bra-
si - cut lo-
cresc.
marc.
f marc.
mf
34
B
si - cut lo - cu - tus est in se - cu - la, A-bra-ham et se-mi-ni e-jus, A - bra-ham et se-mi-ni
cut lo - cu - tus est ad pa-tres no - stros, A-bra-ham, A - bra-ham et se-mi-ni e-jus, A - bra-
cu - tus est in se - cu - la, A-bra-ham. A - bra-ham et se-mi-ni e-jus, A - bra-
ham et se-mi-ni e - jus in se - cu - la, A-bra-ham, A - bra-ham et se-mi-ni e-jus, A - bra-
cu - - tus est ad pa-tres no - stros, A-bra-ham, A - bra-ham et se-mi-ni e-jus, A - bra-
ff marc.
cresc.
p

41
f espr.
e-jus in se - - - - - - - - - - - - - - cu -
f
espr.
ham et se-mi-ni e-jus in se - - - - - - - - cu - la, in se - - -
f
f
ham et se-mi-ni e - jus in se - - - - - - - cu - la, A - bra-ham et se-mi-ni
f
f
ham et se-mi-ni e - jus in se - - - - - - - cu - la, in
f
marc.
ff marc.
ham et se-mi-ni e-jus, se-mi-ni e-jus, se-mi-ni e-jus in se-cu - la, si-cut lo - cu - tus
41
f

47
C
ff
rit.
la, in se - cu - la, A-bra-ham et se-mi-ni e - jus in se - cu - la.
ff
- - - - - - cu-la, A-bra-ham et se-mi-ni e - jus in se - cu - la
ff
e - jus in se - cu - la, A-bra-ham et se-mi-ni e - jus in se - cu - la.
ff
se - - - - cu - la, A-bra-ham et se-mi-ni e - jus in se - cu - la.
ff
est ad pa-tres no - - stros, A-bra-ham et se - - mi-ni e - jus in se - cu - la
47
C
rit.
ff

12. Gloria Patri

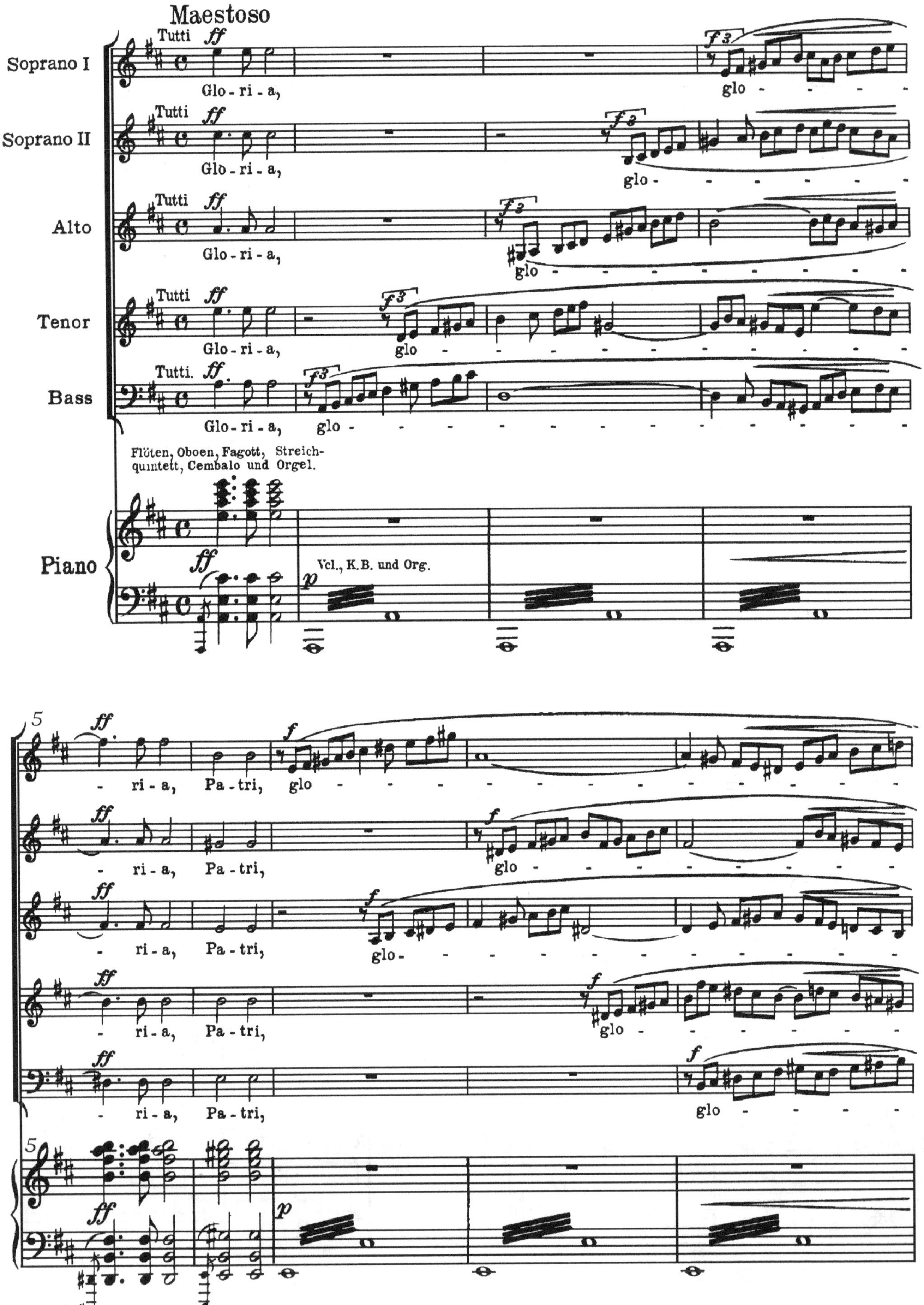

10
f
-ri-a Fi-li-o, glo-
-ri-a Fi-li-o, glo-
-ri-a Fi-li-o, glo
-ri-a Fi-li-o, glo
-ri-a Fi-li-o, glo
10
ff
p
15
ff
ritenuto
cresc.
fff
-ri-a et Spi-ri-tu-i san-cto.
-ri-a et Spi-ri-tu-i san-cto.
-ri-a et Spi-ri-tu-i san-cto.
-ri-a et Spi-ri-tu-i san-cto
-ri-a et Spi-ri-tu-i san-cto.
Tutti mit Tromp. und Pauk.
15
Tromp.
l.H.
cresc.
ritenuto
(tr)

20
Allegro moderato (Tempo des ersten Chors)
ff
Si-cut e-rat in prin-
ff
Si-cut e-rat in prin-
ff
Si-cut e-rat in prin-ci-pi-o
ff
Si-cut e-rat in prin-ci-pi-o
ff
Si-cut e-rat in prin-
20
Fl.
Ob.
f
Tromp.
ff
Org.
f
Vcl. u. K.B.
24
ci-pi-o,
ci-pi-o,
si-cut e-rat in prin-
si-cut e-rat in prin-
ci-pi-o,
si-cut e-rat in prin-
24
Tromp.
Fl.
mf
Str.
f
Org.
Vcl u K.B

si-cut e-rat in prin-ci-pi-o, in prin-ci-pi-o, et nunc,

si-cut e-rat in prin-ci-pi-o, in prin-ci-pi-o, et nunc,

ci - pi-o, in___ prin-ci-pi-o, in prin-ci-pi-o, et nunc,

ci - pi-o, in prin-ci-pi-o, in prin-ci-pi-o, et nunc,

ci - pi-o, in___ prin-ci-pi-o, in prin-ci-pi-o, et nunc,

nunc, et semper et in se-cu-la, et in se-cu-la se-cu-lo - - - -

nunc, et semper et in se-cu-la, et in se-cu-la se-cu-

nunc, et semper et in se-cu-la, et in se-cu-la se-cu-lo - - -

nunc, et semper et in se-cu-la, et in se-cu-la se-cu-

nunc, et semper et in se-cu-la,

35
A poco a poco stringendo
lo
lo
f
et in se-cu-la se-cu-lo
fff marc. molto
35
A poco a poco stringendo
ff poco a poco cresc.
39
fff
ritenuto
a tempo
rum, A - men.
39
Tromp.
ritenuto
a tempo
fff

www.ingramcontent.com/pod-product-compliance
Lightning Source LLC
Chambersburg PA
CBHW081600040426
42445CB00014B/1778